SELECTED POEMS
1936/1966

By the same author

MEMOIRS OF A PUBLIC BABY
LOWER VIEW
STEINER'S TOUR
LIVING IN CROESOR
VAGRANCY

PHILIP O'CONNOR

SELECTED POEMS
1936/1966

JONATHAN CAPE
THIRTY BEDFORD SQUARE
LONDON

FIRST PUBLISHED 1968
© 1968 BY PHILIP O'CONNOR

JONATHAN CAPE LTD, 30 BEDFORD SQUARE, WC1.

SBN 224 61253 0

The extract from the poem by Herbert Read printed below the Dedication is reproduced by permission of Faber & Faber.

PRINTED IN GREAT BRITAIN
BY RICHARD CLAY (THE CHAUCER PRESS) LTD,
BUNGAY, SUFFOLK

Contents

Introduction	11
To the Philosophers	15
He Rides through the Thundering Tides	17
They Came Across that High Rock Collection	18
Le Potage	19
Slays for Love	21
The Shah	23
The Butcher Shop	24
Shells	25
The Murder of the Prostitutes	27
My Aunt	30
Abdicating Reason	31
Merrick	33
Captain Busby	34
Three Poems	38
The Blue Lion	38
Down the Shute	38
And the Exquisite Bells	39
The Baby	40
Told to Shun Monkey Dances	41
The Clock Ticks On	43
Blue Bugs in Liquid Silk	44
Fag End	45
The Raspberry in the Pudding	46
Useful Letter	47
Pages of Irony	49
Whispers at Night	51
Money 1	53
Money 2	54
Love Poem 1	55

Love Poem 2	56
The Tree	58
Modes	60
Philosophical Notes/or Taoist Measures	62
Four Poems	65
Square Ham Grilled for Proletcult	65
Notes (Piano)	66
The Genius	68
Legend of Lao-Tzu	69
Poem on Self	71
Writing in England Now	79
Utrillo	81
ME: What British Christians Can't Know about Egotism	83
Nonsense If You Please But Sense If You Don't	88
Three to C.C.	92
Charlot in Prosetry	92
Charlie in Poetrose	93
Ode to Charles Chaplin	94

Acknowledgments

Robin Skelton suggested that a selection of my poems should be made – who was I to disagree? I merely wish to point out that if he hadn't so suggested, this selection would not have been published.

Many of these poems have previously appeared in the following periodicals and anthologies, and I am grateful to the editors and publishers concerned for permission to reprint them:

Twentieth-Century Verse, Life and Letters Today, New Verse, New Verse Anthology (ed. Grigson. Faber, 1939), *New Apocalypse, Straw in the Hair* (ed. Kilham Roberts. Bodley Head, 1938), *Wales, Poetry of the Thirties* (ed. Robin Skelton. Penguin, 1964).

I also thank Arthur Upfield and Michael Hamburger for their help in tracking down copies of many early poems; also Ruth Elias for copying poems from periodicals in the British Museum: only friendship could justify this chore.

P. O'C.

*Dedicated to Herbert Read
with admiration and affection:*

Persevere through despair.
If in danger
faith is maintain'd
the instruments of attainment
form in a furnace
fiercer than war.

The self, passively receiving
illusion and despair
excluding
the unreal power of symbols
the false shelter of institutions
returns reluctantly upon itself
grows like a bud
petal by petal
exfoliated from an infinite centre
the outer layers bursting and withering
the inner pressure increasing
seeking the light
and the flush of colour born of light.

The root deep in the dark soil of the past
but deeper in the unform'd future
is folded the flower

(Herbert Read: 'ODE Written during the battle of Dunkirk, May 1940'.

Collected Poems. Faber & Faber 1966)

Author's Introduction

When I was a very young man my life was very wild. But in that framework I was also quite a cool young spy upon the world. Life seemed quite beyond my control; and so, in fact, did thought; and I gradually came to think of 'control' as a very pleasant sensation indeed, and one of the most intoxicating myths of freedom in an anarchic society. The life is now less wild, but the ideas remain unchanged. I mention this because my verse, which I began writing consistently when I was nineteen, may appear to be very 'free' indeed. D. H. Lawrence, who was at that time a strong influence on me, wrote very well about the rhythms of his own free verse, which were not at all arbitrary, he contended – rightly I think. Herbert Read writes: 'The rhythmical pattern corresponds in some mysterious way with the inner feeling, and the rhythm ceases the moment the feeling loses its intensity, its "virtue". But meanwhile the rhythm has captured the feeling, held it in a crystal cage ... We have caught beauty in a wild foray'* ... That is my own experience, and I cannot understand the, to me, gymnastics of a regular verse form which, Auden wrote, gives their own particular freedoms. I use *rhyme* entirely as a joke, and a conventional metrical form appears, when it does, at the expense of that other kind of rhythm about which Read wrote; and therefore at the expense of the kind of meaning served by that rhythm.

Actually the matter is not quite as simple. I think that a conventional rhythm will appear in basically rationalistic work, which means work seated in, even if differing from on vital points, the contemporary ideology – which always means in *substance* general conceptions of the rational. Because the rhythm is the song, the song is the first breakdown to its meaning: and the meaning can run regularly along conventional rhythm through orthodox metrical patterns when that meaning belongs to the general 'prayer' or faith or mode of rationality of its period. When it cannot the meaning is a kind of argument, stuttering, waving, diving, leaping, doing anything to avoid the meshes of the contemporarily ideological net of 'reason'.

Intellectually my formative influences would seem disparate: Nietzsche and communism; in Oscar Wilde you may find a clue to

* 'What is a Poem?' Collected Poems (Faber & Faber, 1966).

their synthesis. He saw, unlike our demagogues, that competition is inimical to individualism, and co-operation fruitful in it. But I had a 'split mind', which is the sensible response to a split mode of living – private and public, psychic and physical, competitive and Christian – and I found the formal accommodation of this in surrealism, the only artistic and literary movement in my time which interested me at all. It was with the aid of surrealism that I developed such technique as I have: to waive the intellectual, moral, rational control in the poem at the moment of my incursion into its 'womb' – to fish, with the bait of one combined sensation, perception into the verbal, pictorial and tonal waters where such things are kept, to bring up the number of catches the poem would endure, and to pack them, when they proved impossibly slippery, in my 'ideological' boxes – but never, never, to fish with the boxes. I like to think that the catch of fish selected their boxes; wherever I failed it is when the box took the initiative. And ideally I would have no box, but an integration. That is how I have never agreed with the emphasis implicit in Mallarmé's precept, that poetry is written with words. On the contrary, in my view words adhere to the vision as iron filings to the magnet; all extraneous selection may result in great wit, profundity, rationality and the rest. But it will kill, or rather abort, the poem. A true aesthetic effect is never at the expense of meaning.

I think this view only explains my kind of writing; I don't really think it constitutes a practicable dogma of how poetry should be written. Modes depend upon periods; ours is split everywhere, horizontally and vertically; hence we use the (apparently convenient, though to me suspect) divisions of conscious and subconscious, etc., which I would prefer to render as primary and secondary conditionings: I do not accept the psychological rationalizations of our social-individualistic encapsulations. Were the traffic free to flow from individual to society without offence and defence the 'inner life' would be *marvellously* aerated. But: I think that today the rational and conventionally ideological is not true. Hence my 'dodge'. It is to seduce reason into the revivifying, cathartic experience of imaginative chaos; to render down reason to its uttermost atoms when it may be in a condition to marry with what, ideally, nostalgically or in essence, it was once united. Or: dragging the magnet of an idea through the waters of words/pictures – which is indeed 'fishing with boxes' argued against above. I hope I don't use my knowledge that consistency is a weapon of offence to camouflage a basic nonsense – a hope which should prove quite a gift to critics. Again – I test a concept in a percept, and do not interfere with their mutual modifications: how to see with thought in abeyance but not out of reach, is the art of mentation as I conceive it. Because the concept is one long history of initially physical and latterly intellectual bullying; and an anachronistic ideology provides *very* distorting spectacles, and a dead one provides blinkers. On the other hand witless *simplisme* co-operates with the tyrant by abdication.

Finally, and least forgivably in our country especially at a time when, accompanying the decline of art we have become most religiously art-conscious, I would not like to be thought serious in that manner. I am not serious; my writing is my playing, but my playing *might* be serious: certainly I have discovered the frivolity of too much of my 'working' – almost as frivolous as the average sociologist or television factologist. England now has much interest in being antimentational *and* intellectual: intellectualism is the frivolity resulting from anti-mentationalism. By that, I mean the sustaining of the concept at the expense of the percept; or, thinking without sensory nourishment.

Can I say more to be critically sat upon? I myself rest, most uneasily, upon British reality; who sits on me sends us both through it. And that is a contribution to the progress of our society.

To the Philosophers

Dear Sirs,
I wish to regret
that it was cold today
but the temperature of my emotion
was exonerated from its indication;
its registration was therefore retarded;
the cold night air walks up my stair;
So I lit a fire.

This sort of thing, in one way or another,
happens all my life.
I wish to protest but cannot wrest
the test of reality from the complex of my feeling
due to a mind that is always reeling
or a soul unpeeling itself of its vestments –
reeling to the world out there.

Now take it this way;

my heart is in the mountains :

or another way :

my cardinal sin cannot be erased : and yet another :
God be praised.

Dear Sirs,

I cannot simper at simple things
and be amazed by complication;
my reactions lack official registration;
the number plate of my Ma was damaged from afar;
my reactions are paltry.

Sirs, look at it this way:

Old Man Ferguson stuffed his pipe
and dealt a flea a feline swipe
and composed without a ditty
an opera for the kitty.

Again:

Breathless while he scanned her face
she charged him for a yard of lace:

and:

Dear Sirs,

I am incompetent to repent into the grander wonders
that alone decorate and justify your blunders;

Sirs – dear –

If her stockings were sheer why are your eyes bleary?

He Rides through the Thundering Tides

He rides through the thundering tides who make appalled motion
over the floor of thought in the winds from the heart
laughing as he feels the soft
gradual vibrations of the bursting grandiloquent foam

his spear whistles risky tunes
bright as an urchin's in a solemn street
his hair applauds in rhythmic formulation
each intelligent pierce of his elegant dart

moody mammoths on rocks
attempt to spread gloom by immensity of sitting
and their putrid eyes turn soaked in blood
and bile continues round their heads
instilling with unceasing decision
forms of fumy execration

but he laughs around the abstract pupil of his eye
which drags a thread from eternity
and his limbs shiver and silver in the intellectual game
of riding on out with a strange sight
for the flow of the historic foam.

(Life and Letters Today, 1938)

They Came Across that High Rock Collection

They came across that high rock collection in the exact sensitive middle
   of night
splitting her with brilliant swords and scarlet mules
frightening us with the noise of the roll of their eyes
with the tumult of their sweat
with the disturbance of their thick hearts
with the rhapsodic play of their hair by gallons of exotic wind
with the sickening movements of their armies of foul vapours
with the thunder of their shouting spittals
and with the holy howl of the earth-shaking movement
of more tonnage of limb than we had ever seen.

My brother was destroyed as lightly as a paper envelope
my womenfolk were eaten as delicately as I have eaten
a quite young starling
my grandmother's coughed-up remains flew lightly like
ash upon the crimson atmosphere
and the little winter sun spanked playfully next morning
the head of my sister stuck on a fence post.

This is part of the untenable thread of the symphony of
life I considered extending a tongue like a scarlet thread
this is the proximate apogee of fruition and beneficence
walking with a long step over the holy sky
this is the salty intelligent irony of delightfully wayward fate

of an eternally amusing eternally faithless prostitute called what
   happens

that in a day my heart should be unmoored and my
brain unbound from human society
is a thing I dote sweetly upon in company with this wild rose.

(Straw in the Hair, 1938)

Le Potage

Freud's soup was given to Mrs James; her son
contradicted that aspect, and suggested
through the wands of his mouth that had it been given
to a sign (not a person) the dustbin would not have been
regaled. Therefore :

all actuaries who,
placed upon a green island,
give truth the better measure
need not, like Freud,
have given soup for pleasure.

No steam of this kind can lie upon the emerald air
without its being regretted
by waist-coated men of old; and no air, other than emerald air,
can, with finger on pursed lips,
disclaim with truth a wider knowledge than is held,
in bond and common,
by contributors, arduously, to weekly journals
of good fare.

It is excellent to eat but not to drink
the freud of Soup who, by learning and acumen combined,
brought ruin to an Empire of religious dream.
It is excellent and kind when wantons without faith
parry the faith of an omnibus without inquiring
(out of the left shoulder) the shouted name of its number for :

that number, those digits placed
by scrutable hands on the blinding front
of the roaring vehicle when it was stationary
represent, and present even again a sediment – a seed –
a signal smile that life is not with greed; that handsome sums,

like handsome men,
need not travel alone.

I well remember upon a parking day being sent to England
to recover the way and, one day, wandering upon Blackfriars,
(which is now being consumed by liers who lie rhyming on
the dirty banks of the Thames near by)
met a *Times* in rich human portmanteau, of high income
and girthy tooth which, flashed by the sun, escaped
out of sorrow into sin, down the First Leader.

That was nothing; an experience due to a falconer.
But later (when Brecht had discarded the soup of Freud)
having occasion to enter a bank by the handkerchief
of my losing ideals (which went far)
I established an escheat and compounded with clerks
to *redeem* the saviour upon the cross, by means
of large sums of money. Yet again through this dream there
spread, dusky through the freuds of Soup, that number on the omnibus
    which,
arriving from islanded actuaries,
did in fact change our religion.

But I now have no faith – !

Slays for Love

Rose at dawn, assembled,
rumbled down to the valley, unlocked the smithy's cavern,
foot placed and replaced to the end, stands, arm up and clenched fist
saying smitingly : he took her whom I've loved
in the coil of these stormy arms. I must kill him
to adjust myself intellectually. Else my braincover will leak
with dreadfulness from the sky. (Sky to brain the wizard raindrop
    jumped,
squatted in a carved place in the brain he harried
with lots of cunning tools. He did it at night.)
Drinks Beeno the life-saver, more, the gigantic-making
appurtenance of a would-be well-equipped hombre
given to slouching the world over, and hat askew and trailing eye –
Ware, ware, the super, livid slickey riles
along this swollen way at this time under this sun. Such was he
on taking Beeno, ho, not for ladies Beeno!

He edged his blood to his muscular places
so that they immediately curled up with ire.
He held them in check with an iron jaw, which he carried,
unchanging, unrelenting, to the man that made him cuckold.

This liver stood sweating by his cottage door
clothing his heart with sorrow and fear, well-draped, flounced
and ricocheting to more and more places, lacing his susceptibilities
with more and more expensive, fanciful, virtuosic extravagances
of a libido in guilty slaver. Help, Anna,
he will kill me surely as I stand
a leaf of sorrow and remorse at my cottage door.

High as the night climbed the avenger's fist, disappeared and speared
the sick moment with a downward lurch, and crouched
in the fluid wreck of the adulterous face.

Beeno he advertised to the expectant landscape,
and he took her with triangular leer, a lurch,
an incidental spit that looped around a rose-stem
like a necklace round a lovely, unforgettable memento
of the deed of my hombre.

At dark still – he went home
with his loved one across his shoulder. Make her quick
my reliable nag he said to Mackenzie, his horse,
and his nag swallowed the road like a born toper
of such stuff, didn't dilly-dally, loved the night
as animals do who have been domesticated, and
made it in good time. Ah, descend
incrested lights of night in volumes
of rich delicacies upon me (and my bride).
Warm me in you, reliable night
eternal lover. I, who am a One,
love you passionately. I shall never forget you.

And I rode like lost pus stunned by modern air
to the clothing loveliness of a satisfying deed – accomplished it,
and muscles purring, fawning in me, singing to me
as I returned with
Anna whom I love, like the sky being in my heart
and she the bright bird somewhere sending squinting cataracts of
    melody
up and down, and all over to fill this prisoned sky –

Do you say I don't love you, I,
with Anna leaved by me like a flower I encourage you to grow
and exult and adorn the big silence of life?
No, my brother – who reads –
I love, I have the feeling in exact reproduction
of the leaf of flashing motions in a wind,
of a flower knocked to a million-petalled likeness in a rapid dance
in the wind. I have the feeling
of expiring into the rising, majestic,
stinging, flooding strength of life. Resultant
of our bravest vision!

                                        (*Wales*, No. 5. Summer 1938)

The Shah

The shah
        benumbed cats slide over the lawns
        like streaming music
enters
poised on what o nothing in this contemporary world
the forms of his garden move
bulbs of wishes and swaying balloons of unrealization flock
darkly about him they pray in the dark

their blue prayers in little fleets escape
into the heaven-flowing music's seas
an orange flower still burns like an old lamp
and a violet like smoke in a black rug

the shah perspires wishes
and prayers
unfolds regrets rests
on the waking dream

shadows coolly lie on his sensitive brain
darkening thought and washing with cold sound
him on the ground.
                    (*Life and Letters Today*, March–June 1937)

The Butcher Shop

I enter with tassels and curtains
in cloaks and enormously coloured clothes
in a stupor flabbergasted demanding
Steak and bones and fat.

He has vacated one space
he has jumped into another and been translated
with little shrieks of joy
rapidly to the man chopping flesh

like a storm on a dark autumn evening
is the row of the blade on the bone and the rush
through the flesh and fat like a great train
entering Charing Cross station.

(Life and Letters Today, September 1938)

Shells

In vacancy the skull
gives passage to the shells
and the shells sing to the skull
of the sea's angry peace

and of the sea's great age of knowledge
in men's minds.

The skull is vacant
of lover and fighter,
leased evermore
to shells, wind and shore
who blowing like a transport
of music – which is the shield of the mind
against time –

clean him for his last beauty,
bright bone on the shore.

His brow is arched
for the naked truth
come to rest when immune
to the uses of men.

His mouth laughs
for centuries and skies
an heroic, fixed laughter
scraping, like murder's shriek,
the stars.

Shells
are rolled in the brain's cavity,
knocking for orisons
of eternity
and the pity
of evermore.

Shells
linger
to bones;
in the seas' roar.

The Murder of the Prostitutes

A meeting of the bought and sold –
drearily enough and often told.
But tonight the hellish disappointment at military inactivity on a 2nd front
was breeding murder in the backward mind of two soldiers
so that when they asked two Piccadilly girls
for themselves at a pound
it was only a profound social apathy
that prevented one scenting death.

Walking and talking –
baying at the moon –
coughing too soon –
spooking –
incapable of the torso's descent to his flagrant hips
and hate breeding on that frontier –
chewing nuts like bricks and gunning out the shell
on to the tired, steady pavement –
the unholy three
cooking in the pot of necessity
fasten the mischief of centuries
even yet unatoned by the 2nd front
on to poor bought humanity.

Quick. I hate you like my thrashed mother.
You are the poisoner of my discontent.
I am hell-bent. – Hard into the paltry frame
of a girl of golden life without a name
the knife has stolen another from everyone.

And the wayward cataracting of lost humans in the night,
night after night, out of its hoarse, ancient throat
so obscenely undoctored
has spelled happenings like this.

The little bug
of Doctor Fear,
the little flea of self-respect
says to two of three
we must reject
tonight's awful happenings
in the mystery, history and glamour of fire.

So like two smockless grannies
they light the newspapers, curtains,
then bolt down the stairs.

And of course one prostitute stays crying
over her friend.
And of course the fire rages,
a flood of bawling horror, an elemental damn
at homunculus the ham.
And it's in this city fire honourably burns
like a pearl in the sea which made her
beautiful Hetty.

And it's tottering
very martially upright
that the poor spawn of history
blunder to the next day.

Curtains of an hour
have lifted for the flower
of life to bloom
in that night's dream. But comrade soldiers
the draft on humanity's too great –
one cannot buy one's faith in life
at the expense of another person.

So, drummers heading the army of progress
tap the lightest taps
as brilliant contacts with the other pole

hidden in the enemy's awful forest, the cheap clothing round his defeat.
And on the bridge of lightning
strutting the poles
man victorious marches on.

(Life and Letters Today, 1942–3)

My Aunt

Yes my darling aunt
the boy laughed hollowly.
Squinting at the blue lights freed
through the lily-fine window, bordered
like him by bars of a straight asparagus traditionalism
and even perhaps remembering the wire-flower
of my aunt's hand
subtly cleaning with moral lechery.

Yes my darling aunt – whose
laughs are for ever expressed in the glassy chandelier's tumble
and where principles would beam the ceiling well
and whose ignorance walls us in
papered with playful nosegays
of our *strange* education. (My aunt
is laughing like bits of paper
on a real swanky toboggan!!
Her rippling foolery
is shooting her to war! She's
crashing through,
into the bulging chill water!)
She's smacking down into the madness she's skated on,
breeding rock-chilling militant beliefs
and plans of disastrous action.

She's letting in the young blond nephew –
he's stuck to the teacup, he's grasped
by the hand of her chair
and the room is aloud with the maddening fiery
torrential eyes of AUNT EMILY, great dragon
of Donne Street sheet-armed to the sizzling hair
and MAKING FOR HIM.

(Life and Letters Today, 1939)

Abdicating Reason

Abdicating reason gathers her long wings round her elongating body
for flight,

while her face grows mauve in light.

The responsibility is too great. Emotions have broken through the
floor of her apartment; the drainage from sexuality is blocked; an
idea is wild.

The drums in the town are beating fast in celebration of her imminent
departure. Red flares are quickly illumined everywhere.
Only the children are alarmed, with their very clean faces for
the party they do not understand; could reason catch a glimpse
of them ... but she is shut in her apartment, ready for flight.
God already prepares for his return to that apartment.

One day a flower fell and reason sobbed; emotion backed her up
treacherously, and sexuality came to pour fire on the wound.

That day the madmen's tents were rising on the green, with gold
pennants (banknotes!) fluttering from the top. They said reason
had better see to it. The children admired at their own risk,
and parents knew no better.

The elected priest now beats the gong, which is felt in every
trembling diaphragm, to which rush dregs of thought
and flattened beads of emotion; sexuality is grumbling
powerfully, not yet let out.

A trumpet of folly blares announcing the New Age. Reason hears,
casts one look out of her small window and slowly raises the
roof of the apartment, and like a ribbon on edge flows safely
upwards. As she looks down she sees the white faces of the
cleaned children, in the party they don't understand, and she

thinks they're flowers, now, quite the opposite of dropped.
She laughs and rises ever higher,

and becomes the meteorite that the priest foretold.

There is no moon tonight.

Merrick

Merrick decided the staircase was to be descended by not pulling it
   up and falling graduatedly on alternating feet on regularly
   changing levels, as intellectually as ever; but Martha

was in love with a ladder hanging out of her bedroom window. She
   espied
it by half-light, lattice-like, threaded through trees a bit,
and not a bit frail, so up she went; their meeting

by the Camerons (retired couple) was good. That night, when all
   had nearly gone to bed, Martha

and Merrick decided to meet intrinsically by candlelight, which can be
   shut tight against the night for flight from it.

Yet they didn't care for what they saw in each other – each was too
   worried, too old, too dead nearly, and they blew the flame out.

Captain Busby

1

Captain Busby put his beard in his mouth and sucked it, then took it out and spat on it then put it in and sucked it then walked on down the street thinking hard. Suddenly he put his wedding-ring in his trilby hat and put the hat on a passing kitten. Then he carefully calculated the width of the pavement with a pair of adjustable sugar-tongs. This done he knitted his brows. Then he walked on thinking hard.

2

Captain Busted Busby frowned hard at a passing ceiling and fixed his eye upon a pair of stationary taxis. Suddenly he went up to one of them and addressed himself to the driver. He discharged his socks and continued whistling. The taxi saluted but he put up with it, and puckered a resigned mouth and knitted a pair of thoughtful eyebrows.

3

M. looking out of his window with purple curtains saw Captain Busby thoughtfully chewing a less impatient portion of his walking-stick unostentatiously against a lamp-post. The road was blue but Captain Busby seemed a very dark green with ivory face (for it was night time). He frowned. He looked up to the top of the rapidly emptying street. He cut his hair slowly. He looked at the bottom of the street. He made rapid measurements with a pair of adjustable sugar-tongs. These he afterwards secreted in his trousers. He then flew into his friend's apartment through the willingly opened window.

4

Marcella waited for her lover outside a public house known to both of them. Immediately Captain Busby appeared holding a woman in his arms. This wasn't true thought Marcella carefully, and was

relieved to see that God had thrown a lamp-post at the Captain,
temporarily disabling him.

5

He arranged himself in sugar and put himself in his bath
and prepared to breath his last

his four bottles lay grouped around him

do your duty in this world and gather dividends from
the dog thrown at you

goodbye my children

and he died and they huskily nailed down his coffin
and put it in ten feet of sod
and grouped around him reading the will

for indeed and for ever would he be
to them
just dad

6

Mother lay crying in the withdrawing room
bitterly bewailing cruel fate who with a flick of his pen
had so completely shattered the even tenour of her ways

sobbed upon the brick platform shaking her fist at every porter who
    passed
declaring cruel fate who with a flick of his pen
had so cruelly broken
the even tenour of her ways

7

she considered the porter with the cap on the side of his head fitfully
who had squandered his sweet-peas upon her
who had ridden every train and blown all whistles

to feast his evil frontal eyes on her to break the even tenour of her
    ways
she shunted her back to him
she put on her large black hat with insolent vulgarity
and deliberately smirked into his face

he was busy
he was doing his duty
he rattled the cans
he gave out composed answers to the backchat following his curt
    commands
he went on with his duty forgetting
that he had broken the even tenour of her ways

She walked thoughtfully upon a sugar-box
and would there and then have harangued the station officials to
    compel the attention of the porter

but he did not
but he could not
but he did not
and could not should as he had broken the even tenour of her ways
she thrust a carrot into his face
he gravely took it and handed it without moving a muscle of his face
to the dominant personality of the station
the station master himself
events moved indefatigably to their long-awaited climax
the station master seized the carrot and conveyed it to a drawer
reserved for matters of importance
and seizing a document asserting his credentials and authority
motored along the platform and alighted at the lady

madam he said coldly
your carrot is in the drawer
pray come for it or suitable measures will be taken to enforce
the union of yourself and the personality
who broke the even tenour of your ways

lightning juggled above the station portraying its grim battlements
thunder crashed upon the assembled people

she threw three flashes of self-possessed rays
at him from her large radiant eyes
she ran to the drawer refusing the automobile
she snatched abruptly at the carrot
scenting with inexorable female intuition the precise position afforded
    it by reason if its pre-eminent significance
she ran from the room like a bitten wounded thing
and fell laughing upon the station master who had broken
the even tenour of her ways

Three Poems

1. The Blue Lion

The blue lion poised upon the congregated currents caused by an express
 train
showed golden tongue in the moonlight
and barked

she's frightened within
powders nose delectably and moistens lips
and blue eyes limp over the wheels

of the shuttlecocked train on whining wheels
morose beneath the slippy mass
passing as racing-horses galvanized in steel

my hat holy on my head
such peeping thoughts round the man
my closed shoes bless my feet

or street in the air for the hale blue lion
serrated teeth bashful before the polishing moon
too bright
but gold of tongue

2. Down the Shute

Down the shute whose sides
are black feathers screaming with the fright of my dream
goes the bundled heart
to a white bulb blooming on the bottom

gather in your robes
streaming like hair in the bitter draughts
rolling deliriously in the flight of your fall
bind your limbs to you be a helpless thing
falling to this bulb and fundamental

laughing like the spilling of wine
bathed in my shrieking skin I impinge upon
the air down to the glowing light's node

3. And the Exquisite Bells

And the exquisite bells
long strides of conversation
above spectrally
meet in my brain in blue apparel to continue discussing
the dark
with probing sounds

you said you could
continue to weave in many-coloured streams
soft as saliva
going in and out among the bells but

through bones the stiff tube train crashed its tunnel
through goes like a beam of liking the bright-lit
talk-filled chain of trains down through
to the cloak-walled room of bells and you in

(Life and Letters Today, September–December 1937)

The Baby

The baby should have oranges,
which would run through him nourishingly.
He would then make more noise,
we would wash him, he would shine like silver spoons.

Perhaps he is ill
from the scowling windows. They should be
clear like air to let sun through.

This is impossible. Bag
after bag of soft
dirt
could be collected out of London air.

He should breathe, live,
wave his arms well and show extremely white teeth
among pleasant smells
and moving currents
of fresh air. This is impossible. He will mumble,
whine, clamorously cry. Go white
like bacon fat,
smell like a urinal,
play with dirt, gobble cheap food,
have crooked legs and too-staring eyes,
fall easily and hit viciously, gun like a wolf
and leap for food,
suspiciously cater for himself. This is inevitable.

(New Apocalypse, 1940)

Told to Shun Monkey Dances

The Leader
on the balls of his feet stood up like a nail
while his eyes received the multitude.
In a minute they felt cloudy with silence,
down to a young boy satisfactory as a box
receiving the label on a beaming breadth.

The Leader, fluting his form to a dancer's
exclaimed brickly upon the children. His finger
like the tongue of an adder flames and vibrates
spitefully,
hordes of pins shower from his eyes
and his wiry hand protracts thin fingers
circularly
like a noose. Dumb and buzzing the little boys fear, and creep their
    skin
into their clothes, weighty and wet under their laid-out hair.

Monkeys are brown and intimate, dusty,
skinny but prancing
and devilish as mustard – spits the Leader
in a white frame of Right.

Monkeys touch, then electrically
shine like dirt from the travelling tree branches,
are ultimately cunning and kiss and caress
and are lunatics held
in the snakes of the trees. Bound
by dumb nature
they crackle with dirty life

At night under a hot sky they dance filthily.

They clutch! Bickering with glamour
they totter off and return
riveted to mix.

BUT:

White dolls crisp in the frost of an Aryan regime
will move particularly accurately
in the expression of their joy of living.
The chins, moons of honour,
morning medals
will symmetrically countenance the displacement
of the brother-dancer.

The brilliant hair
will be like hordes of seagulls diversely following
the certain steamer of the Leader.

Unlike humanity
limbs will tinkle to
wisely applauded
drastic and sensational changes of position.

His eye alight
with the true modicum of approved fire
this constuctive mover-of-himself
will be on top of a mountain of trifling
cost to the state. My umbrella above me
I will leave you
to the foregone conclusion of agreement
with my correct statements.

(New Apocalypse, 1940)

The Clock Ticks On

The clock ticks on; the wild-fingered hand
of a dark wet evening strokes the face
and combs the hair out-of-doors,
and traffic and expressions are woof and warp
of a cruelly clear understanding. The people drag a train of
ancient monsters,
cumbrous shadows with banners
of factory hours and weekly wage. Sirens of contempt
whistle in the incidental phrase
and the metre of a force to impel a change
gives words the white outline of chairs seen in fainting,
here we have a room of drastic furniture waiting the re-
mover's approach (and he comes solemn as two girders
in a bridge,
intent as the dead timber floating under it).
No foaming running cloud of the night
can disengage hysteria locked in the pounding heart
slowly rejoining the serene wide-open eye.

(New Verse Anthology, 1939)

Blue Bugs in Liquid Silk

blue bugs in liquid silk
talk with correlation particularly like
two women in white bandages

a birdcage swings from the spleen of ceiling frowning her soul in
large wastes
and a purple sound purrs in basket-house
putting rubies on with red arms

enter the coalman in a storm of sacks
holding a queenly egg-cup
the window stares and thinks separately her hair impartially
    embankment
to the flood of her thought in motionless torrent
roundly looking the ladies

there is no formula for disruption of pink plaster
or emotions to bandage the dead

(New Verse, 1937)

Fag End

The drips surprise. They talk too loud about death (the flanged wheel
brimming with steel that chuckles;
flings glittering eyes on the soil
and shakes the very trees).
The drips creep on as statesmen creep on
in the shadow, pawing every obstacle
and peering for goblins while a parliament house
holds her wide arms over and a clock strikes boldly 5
and shrieks rigidly banging the norm to the quiet people;
say to these arms: Turn
upon the creased mud, slums, and the crafty human structures
negotiate the obstreperous train of drips as well
as the great laws, like charging umbrellas
thrusting through the doorway
sprinkled with the radiant names
of our wine-eyed rulers (one who tosses his fringe of hair back
when he drinks his soup on a mellow table)
Sing like a wheel sing from a mad chest
drunken hearty looking at the puddles
over the gangways of smoke from night to slumdom
and twirl your sunshade to hide
your blond strawed skull from the white
multitude of drips.

(Twentieth-Century Verse, 1938)

The Raspberry in the Pudding

The man in the red scarf comes – from 5 split places
sudden appeared within the flares,
gold lamps and woven songs of tramways. These songs in his
head move around,
with their one sound's finger here and fingers there, above has cleaved
    with crooked light
the spitting lightning,
as this could be a storm and all.
His pantaloons are flying below like movie films so
bright
and their light so changing in interest – very wild, stormy!
and it is electric,
that twitch of his bright white ear
and curved and wind-moulded drop adaptable as water
to your mound of sounds. Down the steep road with coal-
shine comes
the startling and laughing man of the moment – a cinema door
has perhaps spat him up from where the organ draws rising hills – or
a clinic, fussy and epigrammatic, or an awful dome
on a large church like St Paul's.

Never mind. Rising, falling stomach of mother the doomy mind,
though large and wide and preposterous that years push along
adding coating
of sleep or comfort. That loud man of the moment
is late or conceited or takes the wrong turning or is quodded
for not paying his bus fare;
be sure as the turning of a very strong wheel
you will not see him come any nearer. He is a sensation,
for newspapers and headaches. He is exploded!

                                              (*Twentieth-Century Verse*, 1938)

Useful Letter

You mustn't take in more idealism than you usefully digest. It's
like this –
these fingers, that gallant
compact head and the flowing hair that's just frittered away on
    useless
trifles like the wind or an allowance of sunshine.
Everything has its place, like the charwoman in her box of essential
clothes and qualifications or the gentleman poured down *his*
sartorial chimney.
And that necromancer; the baby with chuckling digits gurgling round
a new, splendid, *shining* gadget released from the dark storm.
Allow their minds,
my brother in prison
with the hair-steel bars
launched into this pitiful world.
Allow their self-absorbing drama of
foibles. The stuffed liar, Personality. How deliciously it trickles
on the slopes of chaos – how pretty.
Rain, gentle, wayward on the ruins. I see the Character dribbling his
    charming self on a shudder-
ing city. I see him ensconced on a throne of the past right in the
midst of, no doubt honouring *us* rubbish-heaps.
Long live these resilient blades, my demon.

There is room for everything. The Pied Piper of Hamelyn disturbed
all this – with a magic tune.
Linger in your chair, you
swirling above leprous beauty (chunks of these bodies chaunting,
    performing, flaunting in anarchy, with each
sweaty and tired edge
bidding his partner a nose-thumbing goodbye). I'm sure a ruin
enjoys itself as much as the human plastered assemblages.

A gentleman is a fine thing. I think, you know, he has parts. Yes, I
    have an intuition

(and this only when I am in a dark room with my private African
Congo tribe rioting around) to this effect. Neither, on a sultry day,
 would I be convinced of this
most interesting yet slightly academic

AMONGST OURSELVES

YOU UNDERSTAND! fact. He is mobile. He announces,
denounces, considers. He is struck with an idea, and
about this
my old tomcat (Cecil Rhodes)
tells me he does something. O with certain injury to his health but
how heroic is a gentleman to put up with this and re-experience the
 injury.

All in all my friend to whom I send this letter,
I think there is room for everything and that everything has its place
 BUT you must not take on (be impregnated with)
more ideals than you can profitably digest. No sir.

(Twentieth-Century Verse, 1938)

Pages of irony

1.

… won't furl, even in the brown autumn of a sick life
into brave banners, or even contentive cigars.

We may skate on methodical leers
over the iced pond of the monstrous thing called
reality but must limit, for very fear of our lives
that most sweeping parabola which would take us
over the edge. Over the edge
into
beds of fumes, flare-flowers of a tensile, too sweet
madness: dull aroma.

Dull aromas of sustained chaos, indeed,
and dull aromas in the nauseous preliminaries
of the adequate' and proper life,
before that agreeable death is subsumed in stealth
by the shivering jelly of the reasonable frame of mind.

pages of irony brilliantly scratched
with the newest meanest greenest skit on life
won't furl without the cartoons breaking
into most unpleasant and self-seeming devils;
comes home to roost, indeed, so much of
what we know is wrong with the world. Then oh mercy
what's to do, if the 'adequate' way's a performance in a nightshirt
if the dangerous is a dull aroma,
but achieve a coma as long as it'll last? What indeed?

As long as we're not quiet, as long as one foolish neighbour hears
our cries of despair as long as our tears
can still flow before the internal sob sets in
with its heart-sucking contraction spasmodic to destroy

the heart like a lovely flower minced in the palm of a brute
as long as it is so – well, we are so. Indeed:

2

It had been held by some that the reduction of the English lyrical cloud
into real water would fertilize the country; this is not so,
this was not real.

But we write; we write to write that we cannot write
significantly; we say that we cannot say,
what should be said. Here is our bed,
which should be said; watch how the birds will stretch

their white wings
and fly from it,
how with seagulls' shrieks they leave the house
and wing for the open sea again, where we observe them

through a telescope, a stethoscope, a periscope, a microscope.

Watch how we are captured
by the 'free' movements of creatures and things
unorganized into the social and price rings,
sighing as though we'd once been there;
how we cradle the smothered infant in our breasts,
treat him as the last faithful,
and kill him with love – ungrowing one.

When the stop comes to the expression
the air raves with the unsaid
which may be unlived.

when the stop comes the climbing writer
crawls forward on the bitterly level road.

The writer will find his stop
without his conclusion; such as fate fixes
to the life unlived, the heart unflowering;

though the sun shall rise again for other lives.

Whispers at Night

He slept badly after a congested day
cherishing obstacles for lack of a way,
concocting courage where sense might have said:
'The work of living becomes joy in bed.'

So the departing strands of his mind
in cobwebs littered the room, and unkind
to his daily self-portrait with the best smiles arranged
proposed for some moments to show him deranged.

With occasional rhyme they proposed:

'At dawn when the slate was glassy with rain
and the valley alarmed with runnels of it,
a stone baby that had long been peering at the world
tumbled headlong and cracked his skull
on the bottom.
A sheep bounded away.

'At mid-day, profiting on the event,
a concourse of accepted great men,
sheeny with self-affection and glossy-eyed with mild agreement
with selected opposition
unveiled a new symphonic cloud of incontrovertible statements,
which rose slowly to the floor of heaven
and descended in more rain. We put our macks on.

'In the afternoon of the same magnificent day, a thousand pages long,
the gong sounded for tea; he and she in slender affection
distributed chiaroscuros of intimate dolorosos,
so that the purport of their succinct comport
was to strengthen the acrid rampart
dividing to hold their marital support.

'Yawning then the husband rose for stolen glee
away from the coincidental she;
o yawning and stretching to induce creative retching
of his sticky persona, he climbed the slate mountain at evening,
while the rain came pouring down.

'But rising in the rain to extend
for the sense of existence (simulated) his total verticality
he selected with the two fingers of insane discrimination
a stone, and hurled it to the valley. A sheep bounded away.

'Now we these events are prepared to enter you.'

So he woke. The rain poured hundredfold; the river rose; a groan
  from the skies
preceded a rich clap of thunder; the colour of the night
was a rosy roar, and he turned to his legal whore

and married her.

Money 1

Penniless
upon the strand
of the human heart –
delirious the entry therein.

Penniless –
the round monsters
eat no change.

Money 2

Without money, he says, he stands on the strand of the human heart, seeing that conventionally as an ocean; money would presumably be a boat and the means of avoiding immersion : he says that

the entry into this ocean would make him delirious : what does he want?
Consciousness.

Penniless; he feels his skin withering after his personality has departed. He feels his heart contracting to marble dimensions. He feels frightened of extinction;

£10,000 would have expanded his personality, given him a boat to ride on the human heart like a Brave man, given him consciousness of his own fine shape, and admired it into the admiration of others.

Love Poem 1

Parting from Beloved
means whining for a star,
parting from the glistening eyes
of surprise,
a shut door
from
the baby as big as me.

Howling at the postern,
groaning as the bridge
rigid as a maniac
cuts you off from me.

When you go I feel desirous
of suffering death's greed
and being pulled by his black hands
to my loss.

Darling be my comrade
come dancing back to me.
Enchained ever to each other
is the way we'll both be free.

   (I dress up as they see me
   to rollick in thy gaze,
   even feathers in my cap
   to suffer thy sweet amaze.)

Love Poem 2

Parting from the beloved: the ends of the snapped elastic curled
inward. Their tender extremities withdrew into the thicker
portions of the rubber unextended by the stretch:

Means wanting the brightly unattainable; in this, a vacuum forms
   in, apparently, the breast, drawing the flesh-walls inward:

If the eyes glisten, as they may, with tears, this means a silent
   descent on to the roof of the now deserted sexual regions;
   a no-response to knocking on that roof; and if the tears fall,
   as if the walls accredited to be those of the world fall,
   it is with consciousness alight that he forages in the dark
   mists of unconsciousness:

If he sees that her 'door' is shut, he studies the grain of its wood;
   in the ultra-static situation the grain is vivid;
   if he sees her as a shut door he feels himself shrinking to
   helpless babyhood. She should not have been a house to him:

If he howls, as he says, at the gate – past which a car may carry
   parts of his flimsy identity, leaving a wound when it has passed
   into the distance – if he groans, as he says, at the self-
   lengthening bridge, below which increasing volumes of water
   sing with augmenting power: if this bridge like an animal
   distends itself at last with revolting lyricism, like
   a drunkard's stream of vomit, between him at one end and her
   at the other – its back arched and glistening with enamelled
   curses to his imagined footsteps – if he is left, like white,
   alone: he announces:

When you go I am hungry for death's greed, and I would like to be
   pulled by his black hands to my loss. He then goes mad;
   he says:

Darling be my comrade, come dancing back to me (she is now gone,
   thoroughly, as he sings this in his delirium – he lacks his
   mind): enchained ever to each other (his song continues)
   is the way we'll both be free. This lie is painted

On a vast ceiling of black and gold; the gold, the stars, in effect
   are seething funnels for his blind eyes to roar through in his
   lunatic desire to grasp her, who doesn't want him; and the black
   ceiling, the night sky, is also well below his skin, nursing
   his heart to death with consciousness, which is like riding
   the mountains naked and alone. Passing on, to cure his madness,
   he dresses in it:

I dress up as they see me
To rollick in your gaze;
Even feathers in my cap
To suffer your sweet amaze.

But she didn't see him thus; they did, and laughed. He laughed
   back, and is now a devoted father somewhere else. But he looks
   at her, being blind.

The Tree

An old man was a writer
and searched for his category
and saw a tree.

The tree was obviously
in organic harmony – leaves came,
he meant
not heaven sent,
from tiny twigs and they
came from bigger, which came from boughs, from trunk, from roots;
    said he:
is this a dead kind of category?

And puzzled and frowned.
Felt downed.

Feared he:
was the opposite Something true?

Put bits together
hope for the right weather
and don't worry about organ-ery?

As to say 'They'
will look after ('it')?

He said Shit (contemporary expletive).

No be damned he said
when he went to bed
and they go to bed too I dare say;

the art has a start
in the human heart
and that's in the wide country;

can't begin at the top
for the arty hop
you got not to know what's the start.

Sad having to say
anything of the Way
because it stopped him walking along it.

But times are as bad as they are
though the roads still curl to a star;
yet night-time needs candles on the Way.

He lay down in bed
and to himself said

I'll never be clever by half.

I know art is a tree
and that Fancy is free
that climbs up its branches superb;

I know it begins
to stop all sins
From a centre as quiet as a herb.

Now I'll no more puzzle
my poor works to muzzle
about its nature no more.

I'll now go to bed
with the wife I have wed

and the bravest new world will see More.

Modes

Delightful to play in modes, to use old phrases
Star of all the world and Moon of my delight
to make the clockwork monkeys locked in the zoo of proper forms
fidget in difficult contempt, feel awkward about modes;

delightful weeping in clear Victorian tears
spangled in the daylight of curious modish fears
of those who in the idiom of stiff-lipped understatement
think that statement is so pregnant and flowers impediments
to their pseudo-forthright plainness and their little man's 'tough'
    image;
as though flowers didn't go on holding
all the delicacy of hearts
and stars didn't go on showing
truth as endless beauty, beauty as its mode.

Delightful to resurrect old solaces
such as seas dreaming our dreams in blue
and wearing our heart's lights
in crests of foam and laces dangled from seashore waves.

Nice to see with a curling smile of warmly-held outdatedness
the deep umbrella of the night sky
uncrowding tight minds
of little thoughts nipping each other,
and taking the waterfall for its true purpose
of solving spiritual rheumatism.

Riding birds in the afternoon
with useless thoughts; paying bills
with autumn leaves, millionairing in the sun,
gliding moonbeams of the soul
in water, the breathing dress,
ladling bliss in billows
to shy chilled gollywogs at sport.

When eyes run up trees and their leaves rain rewards
of untemporality, our normal need.

Pray for the brains of man in mortal modes confined
pray for the man kennelled in truths by boards defined
pray for the man praying in chilled superiority elevated
above a world encrusted with the proper thing, no longer elated
by the springing ground.

Who's hoist for evermore to the residence in silence
which is the song of the self's no longer tense
total investment in things of sense;

who feels the gold surging from a pious heart
freed of its religion and its mode;

who feels the golden silence of freedom from the mode
of exploitative contempt; who may resume the forming
of stanzas of ascent
to the firmament.

Philosophical Notes/or Taoist Measures

1

'When you say (a year's leer riding
weekly cops for gain)
centrality's riding peripheral horses
and dies in the Stable of *this* Fame
you're saying – all's outward in a name;
rejecting, you are, the floating population of significance
whose philosophical rendition is fit for cowards only.

I quote:

' – ' Now I quote:

'Not to regard knowing as knowing is the highest
To regard not knowing as knowing is sickness.'

You do not define; you do not define the undefinable
as a definition – no: you sing
in cloudless airs, or cry in grey ones;
you do or think, or whatever
without the shadow of the thing you do or think
in preconceptual hunt of it; you are not wise
to be taken by surprise.

When I saw a copper cauldron I twanged *your* guitar
because yours was the melody; but when my music grated
on your ears, I made coffee,
for what we have cannot apart display
any quality at all but lead astray
its gemlike truth and utter gentility,
which is the flower, the soul, the sweet
of pure utility.

Love,

You.

2

The personal morning dwelt in thee;
thy thigh had crossed mine like twine &
I elongated towards the bed's near shore
and dived on to board, where the trousers rose
like *muflic* garters of the lost, and a whole wardrobe
fell on top of me proclaiming
my gentility, all (them) from view. Gad I said,
Good true.

Power was the room, power her ceiling;
windows bore the fruit of the morning world on planes of dreams
lit blue beside your wandering eyes
my love;

power to the high blue sky and down again
in the rainlike stalks of lights of the morning which we'd
given to the true one-and-you of each other, sister
and brother being the arches making lover;
eschew no name unspat but keep the glory under your hat.

Well I went out on wonky knees
rhyming trees with thees, dear love.

I made my way I got my pay,
gave some of it to you my love :

down the years rolling are the balls of love,
clonking, honking like night foxes and barking
like the geese (to vex police);

good night.

Good night my love; thy name thy body and thy brain
are all translucent concrete coppers of a greater bill
once paid, ensures we'll never again be waylaid
by drunkards crossing the road with garters aflame –
seismic crapulators of crooked existences, such as
official dreams.

Permission is the gold
which the sun accepts
to melting over fields of buttercups and cows;
freedom is the lust of life, and life the diadem;
to permit everything is to achieve the right;
to restrict permission is to achieve a wrong;
our love my love is never spent
on slotting coins bent
into gadgets of prosperity!

Four Poems

1 Square Ham Grilled for Proletcult

Offering	Que je te donne ma vrai belle tranche My people or people or grave simple people de mon coeur bien cuit et mis presque à nu pour toi, frightening, rather frightening, grave 'simple' (no?) people as it were.
Inspection	What's it, a piece of thick square ham wiz emoting juice, well dunked in, with drama-singes wiz tragedy burns an' fat of faith round it trimming nicely, wiz salt o' tears well human brewed, on plate of Life yclept so handsome white unstained a parlour view of royal intruder me an You.
	You offer us this fragrant fare, $2\frac{1}{2}$d single up the back stare of lying eyes, yours do woo but don't really attract, you know. More?
Offering amended	O A'm a gel of high renown sprinkling with beauty the gasping town when I reveal a stocking I show you Life is shocking which is surely how you like it can't you know? Wait look with parsley of me ineffable thought I'll give you what can't be bought faith, that is, ineffable faith, and my soul in plaster of Paris; won't you take?
	Weskered for the public view – no takes?
2nd Inspection	What clothes he wearing?
Claims	Dishevelled like a stripping rose I've paid suffering for this vital pose

                paid down the nose of long Augustan stair
                to paradise of sensual embrocation to show my human
                sweats of evocation of *your* flowers too simple,
                as it were people. O look my clothes are strip
                if entire square are torn surely hip?
                Now don't tell me I've ravaged me in vain –

Rejection He wear his own self-stare, to us he glare;
                blind like all the fat, bemused like patented desperate;
                what he want? To be wanted, a trickster grocer—what he
                    know?
                Don't;
                nakedness thicker than clothes; a wrought-iron agony
                for his garden gate – don't go up his path to hate
                the sight he hates, reflected in his cosmic puddle.

                He's stewed and grilled for many years
                and distilled tears and groaned for ears
                adjusted to sycophancy; he's cooked to shreds
                and his soul from beds with dead companions
                gets up for more necrophils.

                Friends! The stink of the square ham grilled
                is worse than the trotters it walked on;
                the stink of the coeur mis à nu
                drives us even to modesty.

Plaint   Alas, Lock Lomond of my Profound heart
                Alas O drips of dew yclept my bona fide soul
                Have I no hole to penetrate
                with my enigmatic love-hate? I carve you resilient swords
                that me bourgeois friends have forged for Fate,
                O carve me again into dread significance;
                Else how can I earn pence?

2. *Notes (Piano)*

One cold, two knocked,
third coming in
mind; the series rolled

in cold
night; the coffee-stall a fair of heart
20 years gone in Sloane Square, when crawled
from job to revelation, tea : in small things
keep great, root the great.

Matter sweet and sour hard and soft etcetera, matter
foams to mind and mind exhales
in zinc pails every morning as she scrubs
the major ponce's steps who glued to glory
ransacks every titbit whory
with lust of death from which like star-wealth rounds
upon all one note again cold,
freezing in the stewing parts, genital but called still heart.

Ice gold in freezing Galilee
for the shroud of the Lord.

Lord's shroud whose one note I know cold
I do despair of feeling in the live air today – yet
why not? A simple fellow who taught life can be –
what? Can be.

We've produced around one note those beings whose warmth
don't dirt the lunar eye of it; we've made along the years
that drilled an unfelt tear whose purpose
as eyeglass
was fulfilled.

Seen bagatelles and beards! And seen in unrefined reaction
the inner sense of senseless faction;
peace whose one is undisparate, a note
rolled along the columns of the face
of grace; a note called for, culled, still & unstilled,
orb-light, long-beamed, distinct
if born in the sphincter – why not? Gastronomes of proper origins
and deemsters of sin cannot know
that any part has its germane glow;
let alone evil, the corny flower

mussed in the bouquet of the virtuous hour –
– much more than that! Music round a felt hat
is more than that.

Note not the note but cradle
in an agate cradle
the rolling One whose beams erase
the living craze and substitute
beaut-
y.

Matter, myth of wandering pigs
mind, pig of crazed matter; one note
coiled you invincibly
to roll down the columns of the still face
or glow on breast or shine
on dark velvet or be – be :

One note, ice in mind
drenched in the living zinc bucket,
temporarily scrubbing the ponce's stare
of eagerly-pointed futility.

3. *The Genius*

At three he felt a stab of pain
and said I hope it don't come again and
slept well, but they called him a fool
and it came again so he went to market and said
can I park it, yes they said but go to bed and we'll
X-ray for prof. inspection because you know we must have the
real thing, you know, O yes, he said and went to bed

and because of the pill they gave him his dreams were quite
cosmic
so when he woke he knew he had it but actually
they had; well well.

Moral, don't tell.

4. Legend of Lao Tzu (after B. Brecht, trans. by Michael Hamburger)

A story to confirm you:

He (can be called it but it's a man, and what?)
paddled affably in the courtly pool,
a minor pod that talked cod like the rest
and wasn't the best at it, since he didn't invest
preferred rest.

Didn't write a word, humorous he;
didn't want to distinguish him from we –
because he couldn't! Majesty, you call it?
Call it it. Man's it if you shit and you do –
man's it, all there.

Got to sixty, they say, said On my way;
Goodbye Monarch of the Upholstered Glen
I'm past it if it's Zen, which it would have to be
if I married Thee – have always preferred a gentle love
lest I suffer by getting above
it.

It, the Way, and he took its total resemblance –
identical, dear mystic! – you'd stick! –
up to the mountains, wombling along
with his usual leery eery silent song
that made the flowers quite mad to hear
for flowers are mad to those who love them dearly
and never buy them don't you know when –

Hell. A lonely soldier, a sentry guarding what
felt cold and at the sight
of the old man on the old cow (his favourite transport)
(because it got you there without your knowing it)
(it, the way I mean) (and it also)
he felt brilliantly alone. O revelation of
Where's the Path? Or path if you choose, small p
for the weak bladders;

what's guardian said I'll give you bed
(and he said it mainly for the rhyme which still holds
worlds unfurled)
if you'll tell me where; I know in my hut but tell me where
I can direct me paranoiac (dutiful) stare.

Blast said the old man, colloquial like
being too refined to adumbrate
upon the cultural estate
of his refined ex-position (pun)
you too? Like me then.

Okay you want just all I know; so well, though it impinges me
for a minute on hell I'll nevertheless warm me by your
folly, all I respect being in my dotage I respect
your folly, otherwise I don't respect and he wrote:

It goes along by genteely absorbing
what comes to it; if it rejects that rejection
is compelled, like acceptance; it doesn't fuss
one into two unless three or more are in sight;
it doesn't fight, being not loving enough;
it doesn't love, not being fighting enough;
it doesn't gain being rather rich
in poverty not only, dear mystic (*he'll* stick!).

The sentry placed upon his person
this royal philosophical rag and felt hot;
next day old boy goes off, to cool sentry.

Poem on self in form of events as modifiers of self into thoughts to modify the world to modify oneself;

Prologue against Poetry

I ordered cornflakes by note from the grocer with sugar
and various other foods; I drove later to Portmadoc and
the traffic was considerable; I feared all the time as I have all my life
that I would be raped, which set me to thinking again,
as I have again and again, what this self that could be raped
consisted of; and what would result from rape,
and I strove to put into other, expansive words, words
leading to fuller concepts, the together meaning of this rape
as a fact. (Integrity is a word I cannot use – I always say
those who have it allow it to look after itself
and those who haven't worry about it all their lives,
for ever guarding it. One guards only the absent in oneself.)

Putting all this down now I ask me and you: Is this Poetry?
And I have to admit that if it is I do not know what is not,
And if it is not I do not know what is: briefly, I do not know poetry.

This whatever it may be called by professional callers,
a body among whom I am not to be numbered,
is in effect a search for, like indeed so many poems,
like perhaps the majority of poems to this point in history
(when the self remains unsalvaged from other selves
possibly because it is not separate from other selves
and our attempt to separate it
merely reflects our systematically organized
isolation) – is indeed a search for
whatever of self is, as they so deplorably (and advertisingly) say –
unique: I would not like to succeed in this quest. I would like to fail

in order to succeed in a greater quest: what are you, and be led to this
from the point wherein I fail to know what I am.

Is this in effect a prologue against poetry? No.
It is a prologue against what I have come to associate with poetry:
lies arranged by a dead form; dead forms make lies. Poetry as I have come
to think of it is a dead form.

Maybe this belongs to such a form: I don't know; I think
that I don't care.

1

My starting point in life was that I did not know differences,
and my intermediate point was that I failed to make connections necessary
to my nourishment as soon as I saw differences that were alarming,
and my later development was an abstinence from definition
and an abstinence from that abstinence; briefly,
a hopeful dissolution of protective attitudes and mental stances.
I give myself every permission in thought looking never for consistency
and order and never seeking the lack of them.

My starting point in life was that I did not know differences
as 'vital' and to me as alarming
as those known, it seems and seemed to me, to my elders
and above all when the time came to my educators,
who appeared to me to be obsessed (hallucinated) by differences;
I can hear still the typewriter tap of the pedagogic voice
damning phenomena into their differences
and then sodomously allowing in a quaver of mystical defeat
certain 'wonderful' connections.

My starting point in life was that I didn't know differences;
hence I gather that myself was mainly feeling of textures,
such as my mother's skin and textiles and objects,
all of which were solved into a common denominator,
which was I in my creche, my safety

As I grew up and observed and noted such phenomena being sent from
   me
with names like masterful riders taking them across horizons I would
   never reach
and beyond which lay, may I say, the thunder of madness,
I developed an understandable sense of isolation;
for I must insist that phenomena and the skin of my mother
were similars, and I must know that she went with them, as she did.

So I in isolation was an early sensation and feeling,
and very soon an observation; there grew a wider ring around me,
and from me to the ring, to the frontier, lay grey emptiness whose
emptiness being vacuous might if I relaxed
suck transmogrified the departed things and a person.
So was determined the I I conceived, and I have not known another
and in, perhaps, an excessive simplicity, I have aspired to know another
   I,
which I think may not be: Know thyself is Know thy self-conception,
a capitalistic measure of viable hallucination.

I must say that the skin of my mother and her voice
were sooner mine than her person, which I never knew,
and which I created therefore in replica from absence
to guard me when she did not.
I was my mother; how can I fit in those exiled phenomena with her?

I will leave them; they may return.

For I have omitted to write that beyond the horizon to which
exiled phenomena had been ridden away
by definitive riders in armour got from aliens
lay a more detailed world than I have expressed
as the thunder of madness, to which it was said I was slightly prone
by those who identified themselves with the aliens
in order to be safe: to whom they had been frightened as consorts.

I may say that beyond that frontier lay the cattle of knowledge so-
   called,
lay phenomena out of my context,

lay a rowdy bric-à-brac which it was heresy to attempt to understand,
because disconnection and alienation was the faith of the people
from the ordinances of their masters who seemed to be people.

I may say that my lovers, my phenomena,
against which I had proned in the summertime of an infancy somewhat restless,
appeared to me quickly to be almost beheaded, to have had their brains
leucotomized,
to be deadened into the parlance of alien knowledge,
that they were quickly tortured to facts which fed knowledge
which was a machine constructed to mangle our true brains,
such true brains being ever the nestlers in our sweet bodies,
which love informs in life.

I saw that we the children were attached with facts
by educators who wished us to share
their own estrangement from such facts, which estrangement was created
by the murdering of phenomena into facts. For we were little Christs
tortured to give up the world, O Fools, to make of it thus
this sediment of reality, this sludge of existence
so known to you, poor reader.

At school I quavered to hear a fact announced,
I squirmed and sweated to see the approach of this surgical instrument
designed to cleave me in two; but my resistance to this cleavage
was later heralded as schizophrenia : which, dear reader,
is what schizophrenia is : the rebellion against such a division
into the sensuous, around which living mind is clotted,
and abstract fact, which sucks the elixir of life, distilled to spirit.

2

I made me a self to negotiate the grey vacuum vacated by phenomena
which would phantasmagorically return as facts
and by my mother who would phantasmagorically return as the women
who were not she when unveiled.

How to make a self? It is easy, too easy.
Take a pair of sparkling eyes –
take a pair of ruby lips –
take the woman who has gone away
and see her in the daily mirror of your life.

Take the gone one's voice's song
and whisper she is you –
augment, and amplify the portrait.
Cover it with molasses of tears unshed –
carve round it the antique warrior you never saw
(the father whose cosmetic is gore)
and you have a self prone to disintegration.

Strut and prance in the auditorium of your solitary observing self,
play to you, check it and improve it, give it your heart and soul
('he is self-centred' – thus the fools:
he is eccentred, thus I know)
live for it night and day, and find this retribution:
that the player steals the audience
and a dreadful quarrel ensues,
an equivocation lasting half a lifetime,
a quarrel as to who am I;
a tug of war
between wife and whore.

Retribution? Has an answer, as have all questions asked
to excess. Send with a withered secret grin of destructive anticipation
this fabricated player-self into the world – close the theatre
'go' into the world (It goes, not the audience you)
and watch it with delight
be smashed; grubbily stare the strewn parts
of the makeshift player and dare – dare at your peril then say:
the real I is the one who stares with glee
at the destruction of the foundered he:
for this is not so.

Once again I had no I; definition was felicitously removed again.
Now I wonder in the mist

by what creator I'll be kissed; and his name
is surely Everything.

Thus I learned by use of this proxy self
to disregard action until it anchored once again
into me.
I would not agitate, which was to speculate,
which speculation was operated
by the conjoint unharmonious pair
of the allegedly true I and the self-conception.

3

There endured a long time of no-self;
each presumer to the throne
was rejected; in the mirror the face slowly
wore out, and the mask like an empty cake tin
yawned its weary dissolution.

Rejecting all selves within my knowledge
I saw that most of us are in the same boat,
and I could not believe the you of you
equally with the I of I.

To be sundered from all conception of self
needs the prop of disbelieving in your conception of you,
which I saw play with all the lifeless vivacity
of the I of I.

I took for then profound
the dictum of Shakespeare, sent to cliché by uncomprehending men –
that all the world is a stage : which I amend :
all this limited world.
For there's another outside the theatre,
in its animating context.

I lay like oil on water,
like milk on infant's lip,
moved by a satisfying unknown larger wave,
and I basked for many many years
under the sky, avoiding roofs.

One day I would be called to the core, I surmised,
and I became the pilgrim of the call, which silenced it.

Do not pursue what will inevitably come,
or flee what should arrive.

4

In those years I playfully made (avoiding the pundits' grimy reach)
a theory of self, summarised in the words 'anything' and 'anyhow':
know not thyself, I presumptuously said,
and fell to bed in another definition (of anti-definition):
to point which I will quote:

'Not to regard knowing as knowing is the highest.
To regard not-knowing as knowing is a sickness.
Indeed, it is only by being sick of that sickness one is not sick.
The Saint is not sick because he is sick of that sickness.
Therefore he is not sick.'*

5

Later I strayed into the cult of the spontaneous,
which in these unguarded times wears an air of gamy springtime;
but this by eschewing made volition a demon exorcized in madness;
volition to be undermined must be contained;
volition and the spontaneous are a pair to go.

6

When I go to foreign places
and all with people are foreign
because such is this world in which we are made to each other
    foreigners
I fear to be raped;
what is this fear, what is this I?

The rape is conversion by force into you;
the I is the weakness of it constructed in your despite.

              * Tao Te Ching.

As long, dear reader, as we are I against others,
constructs built in a relative difference,
we are prone to rape, to defence, to offence.

How shall I write the new I unborn?

A cliché must serve : as a flower in a garden,
as an individual in a community, whose sap
is everyone's, and the garden of them the world to be.

I can sustain no defence without sickness;
from which I know that we are alike,
from which I reject our patented differences.

True difference blooms without patents,
and its nourishment is commonness.
In a fit of early madness dreaming of the coalescence I sang that I am
 you;
I know better.
To be like you is nearer, because identity is annihilation –
identity thrown at me which makes me try to jump into yours –
fences are the curse of humanity.

So alien are we that only love, that exhausted concoction sweet though
 it be,
can place us within civilized calling distance.

Sometimes when I go to Portmadoc I think of shopping and my family.

Writing in England Now: from a commercially unsuccessful point of view

This poem I write to teach the reader
what I know about writing in England today,
which is a country, England, chronologically,
in no other way,
today, because it is old-fashioned, as *Les Temps Modernes* wrote
in 1964, 'emerging from Victorianism', I think it wrote, 'uneasily'.

This means:
'I' wields a muffin-density challenge
from a poxed centrality shaped like a fortress;
the terrain's abstracted to cartography
to cater for the entropy;
the people is a-Mused.

The able writer hears what he has written being said by people
who of the right sex he wouldn't mind in bed
before he writes it. It gives felicity to his writing.
It makes his challenge biting
to save his readers writing
what they hear is very true,
they pay their servant.

The able writer is a man to himself
and has proved his virility to prove this to himself,
never mind the woman.

The able writer by not agreeing
agrees more agreeably
than by disagreeing; he has a broad mind
to accommodate a changing rate of exchange
of people who said what he wrote
from time to time in bed. This bed may be spiritual. I'm not saying

his attitude is carnal, I'm not saying his attitude and I'm not
saying. But he chooses that view which they said he wrote was true.

The able ugh writer must coo. That coo must be punctuated without
   its stopping.
Punctuations provide the clipped snarl to stop the too sweet.

Writing in England today is like waving the red programme of a
   bullfight at a menu with roast beef on it.
It is definitely transcendental because it writes in terms of solid things
unsolidly. But it writes of transcendental things like dropping cowpats
   & calls this realism.

The rudeness of the able writer in England today is bad breath not a
   fart because it comes from his mouth.
The politeness of the able writer in England today is eau de cologne
   from the fundament,
than which there is no greater part of respect. It is fundamental respect.

I have mangled the lavatory towel of this language as it has become
through the terrified mastications of terrorized journalists
and brilliant, shocking and disturbing novelists
until I think it was toothpaste, and my teeth are black, it was bad
   toothpaste.
I have not respect. I have not money therefore. I want money.
Editor, print this and send me some when you call it a poem
to teach the reader what I know about writing in England today.

Utrillo

You kept the meat but flamed it
in the involuntary air
of faith that this was not
man's life, and by not knowing you derided
and will have helped to distinguish
the world from its bourgeois carcase.

So that meat you gave
the flame of its new bearing
on humanity;

in those physical musings of the poor
called living
in those deep endurances within the frames of another's world
you played the organ of your colours
and you ranged some future human notes
as houses known to man.

Gravity is the heart of joy,
and joy is the mind of progress;
gravity is human endurance
and joy is human development;
gravity is the mother-form
and joy is the flying child
to the places of the sun;
gravity is the womb
and joy the child.

You kept the human meat
from the dust of its cynical purchase,
and you aired it with anticipation
off a synthesis to come;

bringing reasonable heavens to earth
you raised hells for its nourishment:

you knew and showed
what many have known and few have shown;
that the mortal crisis is but the hesitation
of immortality at our threshold.

ME: What British Christians Can't Know about Egotism

Fools!

(British pussies went on sleeping,
to keep a tryst for moral Bo-Peeping
on the sins of others being
what they never could.)

I say to you

(He says to them. British pussies
made him that says to them)

You do not know

(They do not know)

What is self.

(A wild wreath of trumpets sing ha ha;
gladioli of music arise from a wealth
of swamped meadow. White flowers stick
like hours in the green)

Pity.

(Says it's a pity)

Pity.

The self is not the self that's known to the self.
The self is not the self that's loved by the self.
For this is a married pair; one behaves
for the other to stare
till the edge of doom an identity.

Lord, in your days of our hallucinations of your power
you cut us in two, the one to be loved
the other to woo; and it became my endeavour
to wit this woo.

(The owl sang in the belfry of the madman's mind,
who chose the night to see what in the day made him blind;
the world was unkind)

The egotist
is the lonely tourist
voyaged far away from himself
who seeks the road home
which he will never reach,
can only preach
in moments when the fire of brains
rains down in red sulphur like a town alight
the magical trust : I am you.

Hey diddle-diddle
on a one-string fiddle
I am you;
the now jumped over the boon
of time, reason was trapped in a rhyme,
and looking ahead from researches in my head
I discovered, when mad,
that I am you.

Hey diddle-diddle on a one-string fiddle
the show limps over too soon;
down before the Juggernaut
I fall to what I'm taught
tautologically that I am I.

Fools.

(British pussies stir.
They have dreamed they are dreaming,
the light of our island blight)

I will tell you my life.

(They made the he, a blacked cardboard cutout
who will tell them his life)

I was born fair in a fair world.

(He was fouled)

I was left.

(Politically, we dare say)

My mother

(We scream with embarrassment. We cats
can't wear such references, substitute deferences
to things like *that*)

left me and took with her
an 'I' unweaned, and left the mortal packet
like a jacket without man :
for *that*, the world.

As a jacket I wild and waved
and extrinsically behaved
along the trotoirs paved
with good intent, bent to every whim
of every her and him, never knowing
that I was showing
an emptiness so slim
as never to be housed
a form without a rim.

Fools.

(We made him make us in his mind
abusively unkind)

I searched for me down the years.
I washed in tears.
I dressed in fears –
the feathers, wild and screaming
of fears, dreaming, waking,
terrorized by the night
of day.

I became my mother.

(Incestuous brat; we saw to that.)

And searched for my lost one, my darling, my he,
me, me, me. I made me what I am not.
I saw you for what I am;

For it became my mad intent
to wit that wooing
of an absent me; I had to, else –
you would have cured me of my search;
which God, before he died, forbade.

But lo, and behold.

(The pussies wakened;
their tails were being told)

(One by one; the things were being
undone)

Behold!

In this long pilgrimage
along the road of excess
I found the palace of wisdom,
a little shack on a mountain top
which the winds played the tune of my life.

For that shack was what I sought
a self unsold a self unbought

a self without walls or roof
with only an historical frame
of something that might, had I not been lost,
been given a name.

A weary skinny mother
I found my little child,
me, me, me;

and me – behold!

(Behold on to your tails, pussies;
he doth his tale unfold)

Am nearly nothing.

Praise, praise,
the rooftops raze
from the idea in the maze
of our misunderstanding.

Freely, freely, I say unto you

(He does not charge for his good intent)

that the reward of the lover and seeker of himself
is supreme,
is nothing.

So I learned to wit the woo;
he diddle diddle,
pussies can you fiddle
such a wonderful tune
as 'I am you'?

Miaouw.

Nonsense If You Please
But Sense If You Don't

1

The long manner spared no pains
to correct byways of despair,
as the mother of too many orphans
tears her hair.

The manner betrayed some heart-felt problem,
as the mother died from creation;
but the orphans are clapping into lasting life
a father without his hair.
Symbiosis of the unfit
has led to shearing heirs
from the nuptial strands of a million hands
which compose the loved of the lands.

Obsolete our parents are
said the fat voices of the orphans afar
but we too constitute a nebulous neurosis,
a liver's sedulous cirrhosis
volumed, we know, into marbled Stoke Pogis.

Fat though we be
in a fat country
which wise of its wealth
is native porcine
in the waving of its loose body through arches of
social democratic skirts :

fat in this country's eau-forte principles;
fat in the thick-necked speech of its guttering
main political speakers, leaks and cheats;
fat in the damned intellect
in the fraud's thinker articulate;

fat though we be
in a fat country
we too can tell two apart,
we too can kill to the heart
straight-shot: shoot, take it hot
to the ruddy beast who likes it fresh;
i.e., sponsors of Rhode Island Toothpaste,

grinding skilfully the nickered-o'er
shambles of the thigh-ful whore,
like lust in liars' spumy mouths
in the drench of a cabinet me*a*ting.

The orphans, it goes without crying,
were nobbled before dying
by a mouthing poet-willow-tree
shaking his fronds in liquefied daughters;
I see their red tops nodding in the grave
for the wind spared a few to shake them.

2

The long manner's hatpins seem shook;
has the pawnbroker them took?
For what affray, for what assay
can the pawnbroker them have took?

A deed in jet is a prick in lime,
and noble were his teeth sublime
as they scurried through a yard of slime
that made him make those bucks a time.

I make a royal to boil a bob
inside the furnace of a nut of cob;
I make a tree for childs to pee
on a landscape wintry.

For no God in other worries
can condense the snowflakes' flurries
into Indian curries
or skates of glass;

you have meaning in my dreaming if quietly keeping in your coffin of
    green
you appertain to things not seen
other than out of or in the green
of silence by the Weir of Lond
which goes with a carcass cosy in bond.

My mean is this, O reptile space
which with its pash of maths in lattices of space
creeps out a piece of ferruled intellect – they say –
but flops, before it thinks, to pray.

For the long manners were at the end of the realm;
the hatpins were tinned pineapples
of rectangular explosiveness,
maybe pawned or anti-spawned (such those economics);

but the manner is a preying vulture
on the mauvey meat of culture
licking all its heady pus
on the upper part of a sixpenny bus
ride.

In the broker of pawn they spawn bombs from hatpins;
O sirs of Albion fair if splayed,
tell me have you the past waylaid
quite?
Or shall you interfering with your victuals
erect another group of skittles
to play hellfires auspicious in your day?

But Tom but Tom the piper's won
and he's blowing his nose with his only son,
come come the culture's done
don't you know that nobody's won?

Except the piper in a foreign field;
your name is on his shield.

3
The interim is panting to a halt.
The bogus ruler nots his shalt.
A pony is at the gate
made of pure hate – the gate –
but a horse as old as hell or heaven
winged for truth and darted to victory
and soaring like the heart of a thunderstorm
winging, winging, friends and enemies
to the play of the part of the whole:

tomorrow,
grandeur.

Three to C.C.

1. Charlot in Prosetry

A love letter to the world
reaches its destination
if the address on the envelope
is unreadable
by the addressee.

Music makes the powers by night
inflame the heart,
but light has no way of knowing
its light;
its addresses are unseeable,
its luminosity invisible.

Happiness weeps its wealth to see
cast over the pale cloud of husbandry;
but the workman at his toil
finds balm in this midnight oil;
the husbandmen is agreeable.

Your purple chord
from the piano of our hearts
drawn till the wooden framed sobbed
and life itself felt robbed

has been the bruise on my brow;

because the one man I knew I never knew
I never could be;
because genius is the curse of identity
and I never knew I could not be he,
Charlie.

Limping in inferior arts
patching up less purple parts
graduating to contemporary farts
graduating to the insanity

of the sea
and the time, and light above
which draws us from the groove of life
into the heart of the mystery;
Charlot I know I know but, Charlot,
do I know that you are he?

No: Charlot: you
are not – me.

2. *Charlie in Poetrose*

They made a big building by the sea,
ma mère Marie, ma mère Marie,

and incorporated in its heart to see
me, Marie, me Marie,

and flung the wastes of life to shame
on a beach without a name
Oh Marie, mère Marie,

where the trumpets blew all day
at the devil-man at play
waiting for the day
and you Marie, Marie mère Marie.

They blocked the heart in a blue boulder
and said: be older before you meet
your mère Marie by the big blue sea
below the boulder of her house
Marie, blue Marie, vierge Marie;

orchestras come and go,
blossoms I know
fanfares of tears
and new moons of love,
which are smiles.

But they made
that big building by the sea;
I cannot see my blue Marie;
she goes and is gone;
lost, never won;
uncaptured,
distraught;

in the window of my love
I met Marie.

3. *Ode to Charles Chaplin*

By a lake
by a whore
by a tune
and more

wandered a mere phantom
with the egress of a bantam
tailing a tom-tom
to Africa wild
of the world.

A sky encased in a lemon-rind,
a jewel of sight in the milky-blind
eye of a wandering minstrel,
a stick to gird the loins of the poor
and boots to trample history o'er
with the roses of its imprints
for evermore;

dignity slipping at the chalice of grief
money trembling on the lips of the thief

hatred like the ovens of hell
striking the big cathedral bell
and an eye which sees like the world at large
its passage through space like a funeral barge
where bodies unborn and souls unblessed
carry on
to the wonderful shore;

who took the toe of madness
on a genius of gavotte

who got :

?

through.

And the world replied
'I am you.'